A LITTLE NIGHT COMES

✴

Julianne Buchsbaum

A LITTLE NIGHT COMES

✴

Julianne Buchsbaum

— Del Sol Press • Washington, D.C. —

DEL SOL PRESS, WASHINGTON, D.C.

PAPER ISBN: 0-9748229-6-5

FIRST EDITION

COVER PHOTO BY SHAUN O'BOYLE, WWW.OBOYLEPHOTO.COM

COVER DESIGN BY JIM RUFFNER

INTERIOR DESIGN BY ANDER MONSON

The text is set in Minion 11/14.

Publication by Del Sol Press/Web del Sol Association, a not-for-profit corporation under section 501 (c) (3) of the United States Internal Revenue Code.

CONTENTS

III

IV

✦

✦

ACKNOWLEDGMENTS

Grateful acknowledgement is made to the editors of the following publications in which these poems originally appeared:

Gulf Coast: "Beyond Fluorescence" and "Shadowboxing"; *Prairie Schooner:* "Terra Damnata"; *American Letters & Commentary:* "The Power Plant"; *Delmar:* "How Many Cool Hundreds" and "The Unsaid"; *The Journal:* "In Squire Park with M., Esquire" and "Bitmap of Sepia"; *Harvard Review:* "From *The Dialogue of Balm*"; *Denver Quarterly:* "An Écorché of the Continent" and "3 Car Garage"; *Drunken Boat:* "Demi-Vierge," "Dear Introvert," and "Aloof from All the Moorings, and Afloat" (as "Darkness of Proper Names"); *Web Conjunctions:* "Journal of Evenings with Antoine"; *Conduit:* "City of Surfeit/Circuit City" and "Farewell to Finality"; *FENCE:* "Critique of the Metaphysics of Bees"; *Southwest Review:* "Variations on a Theme Beginning with Darkness"; *Verse:* "Some Towns Are Small" and "Flower of the Hour"; *The Canary:* "Dear Beekeeper" and "Flight From Old O-Field"; *The Iowa Review:* "Bomber's Moon" and "Perfect Motels."

"Thrillsville," "The Power Plant," "In Squire Park with M., Esquire," and "Phantoms of Utopia" also appear in the anthology *Legitimate Dangers: American Poets of the New Century* edited by Michael Dumanis and Cate Marvin, published by Sarabande Books in 2006.

My thanks to Shaun O'Boyle for permission to use his photograph on the cover.

Thanks also to the many friends who have read these poems in various forms and to my family members for their support.

✦

for L. R. L.

i.

THE POWER PLANT

Under the copper-clad latticework of the power plant,
you were a mix of vandal and sylph and I waited
in the parking lot for hours. It was easy to vilify,

not easy to fix. In a world the color of lampposts,
it was hard to take to wife and hard to be taken
to wife, season of bureaucracy, season of gleam.

Imagine what we fled into, what the fire became:
bright red flags warning of high-voltage lines run
underground. I imagined what we would become

in the house we sat alone in. Darkness was scattered
everywhere like the hairs of a cat and I told you
a tale of nettles, of the sandman palming off his nada,

caressing your will with null. The hazards were buried
under the corruptions of autumn. Lamps were lit
underground, you said *Hush now,* like a mother, *here*

you are safe. You told me a tale, it was hard to be taken.
The sky was ash and smoke, a man made of sand.
Buried leaves became a bureaucracy, a fairyland in flames.

I was taught, in the parking lot of the power plant,
we're safe here. In the lynch force of its latticework,
you were a cross between mob and aristocrat.

EROSIONAL

Part of you must be forest, swarm,
a way to set the sky in motion. Go

at nightfall to the landfill, O
yellow ether of a mind breeding

nightmares. Blowflies are movements
in the sky, neon flares, yellow

weathervanes. Soon the sky will be
halfway between flint and indigo.

If, in the silence, all the birds
be dead, like a man haunted by

harlequins, slip past mustard-
colored houses & enter a place

of attar, stars, a virus. Think of
nuns, months of seclusion, speed

past picket-fenced suburbs to a scene
of deadwood, rust, and blowflies,

imagine future nights
in apartments filled with flowers

that breathe of rot, the city's founders
silent in their tombs, explaining

nothing, as stiff quills accumulate
in a field of broken wires.

HOW MANY COOL HUNDREDS

Above the obstacle course of the old quarters,
I see the moon and remember Monte Carlo.

All the odd byways and obliquities, an ill wind
unstitching an impasse, a third wheel, stasis.

Zero-lot facades, their squalor and bricolage.
A catwalk extending its skeletal cambered hand

disturbs me. The pathos of potholes.
At the quarter hour I see the quarter moon,

the fourth part of its magnitude on the macadam.
Scaffolding around a half-built house:

I am afraid to touch, I am afraid to let go.
What was once a giddy encounter in a broom-

swept cupola is now a life of lies inside me.
All night I feed my slot-machine while the sky

types messages. *I am a god, rising,*
the chips of blue plastic fly. Deuces wild,

my deck of diamonds, the moon shimmies
down like a dancer in the chuck-a-luck leaves.

DEMI-VIERGE

My tutor's bedroom is cluttered with lectures.
This past week I have shorn my hair,

burned my letters, and in a suit of Harris
tweed I delete all thoughts of mawkishness.

Avid for new vistas, we pay to sleep
on a velvet divan while the refinements

of night are procured at the edge of town
by libertines. Expenditures are endless.

Outside in the greasy sky, oil-colored
birds fly and fly. The phantoms of old

philosophers foul the place with colloquies
on solitude. (By marriage or death, they will

enter gardens.) In posh clubs, we are custodians
of wigs and prostheses, lovers of artifice.

She tutors me among flower vendors,
roving wolves, abandoned Volvos. The fissures

of her lips filled with red, she leaves in hot
pursuit of something ripe by the piers.

TERRA DAMNATA

Every S.O.S. is hexed and I—
dressed to the hilt in the killing style—

forget what the mainland looks like,
how the hooves of ungulates sound on the hills.

Another rank, subversive night, the air
is thick as jellyfish, a swarm of stars.

Only the high-seas glint in the eye
of a lover taking her leave of me says

I am not at this nadir for nothing.
A wind of clove and bergamot beckons

and forbids my turning back toward the inlet
where clouds horn in over cordilleras.

Under a sky white as coconuts from Trinidad
this topography of scallop and lack.

Unrepentant I profane the black penumbra
of her hull—*or was it skull?* One false step

and days become jails. Silence on the wharf,
silence in the rain—*hold still, afflicted thing.*

I am below-decks, drunk on Chianti.
The ship gives off the smell of death and cinnamon.

DEAR INTROVERT,

in the recurrent blues of evening,
all the animals are around me.
The tenements across the river
are only lines carved in drypoint
with a stiletto quill. Their wax back-
ground will surely melt under this sky
banded with the colors of bottles
in barbershops, a sky untroubled by
spacecraft. If you were here, I could stop
wishing you were here. When I was ill,
pallid as broomrape in a clover field,
Lady X came to greet me in a wig,
and we spoke of luxation and accidents
under the tyranny of a pig iron moon,
the era of cigars and courtesans,
the bristling polyphony of Purcell.
As if we could speak a dialect of twins!
On Black Friday, glass facets mirrored
us endlessly where men ate pies
from automats. Distance effaces more
and more of your features. And though
the hours are crucibles I may not survive,
I remain
                —your anti-bride.

BITMAP OF SEPIA

The sun runs riot through a bitmap of sepia,
a landscape where small mammals hurt
each other to stay alive. The sun tunnels
into my small El Greco hungers, dreams
that fluoresce into maids, petioles, feathers.
As the numb hunchbacked earth yellows itself
with weeds, the afternoon buckles inside its stains.
Tranquilized by the tinctures of Lone Tree,
I forget that I am inside those stains, that if
the wind abrades me here where there is no
in-gazing, I'll turn toward meadows where
no one falls in love or with the wrong crowd.

BOOLEAN CONDITIONS

I file away the Boolean *Or* of your love as I file away
the deeds of artists in violence who build states—under L

for logic. I went out walking today to rid myself of these
abysses. I stood at the borderline of an orphan's home, the sky

without the eye of the sun like the mood of a man impugned.
In June woods sticky with sweetbriar, a vortex of black

insects swarmed as if making a dictionary out of small
parts of their bodies—as if the spirit of matter harboring

perfection included the possibility of your frame. I stood
at the borderline of black insects swarming, in woods sticky

with sweetbrier, a vortex of the world. As if their bodies
were dictionaries of foreign words, animals are prolific

in shedding records that contain a secret history of the world.
They are prolific in spite of the grave and everything that's

a chilling repetition of what precedes it and won't be found
in catalogs filed away between the histories of X and Y.

To the yielding of these abysses I give all my heart, as if
not the Boolean *Or* of torture awaits me (*Either Animal*

Or Machine) but a morning filled with sweetbrier.
I never married because the election of love is less major

than the yielding of every type of light to categories
of strangeness going on in silence like a door swung open.

JOURNAL OF EVENINGS WITH ANTOINE

    1.

Sky, you are all thatch, tarry, and strangeness today.
A motel, a tinted money-box. Antoine's length fails
to stir me, yet he makes good his promises and finds
several charlatans pretending to knowledge of crimes.
The phraseology of sages throws dust on my stereo.
From modern dumps, damp modems, come the valentines
of my hirelings. Bats socketed in their moist stoup.

    2.

As if this night could enter my Carnegie heart
or answer these petitions with stars, Antoine slants
in & ignites a change in ions. He does to sleep what
wind does to the tarn. Antoine is anyone who inclines
himself to instrument panels of broken machines.

    3.

In between trips to rabbit island, chaos becomes this
low-speed honeybee. In the space of a week I'm
reduced to tokens, I skirt around the topic of modesty
and neglect my older brother. In the Offices of
Anesthesia, I wake up to a mouthful of rotten teeth
as Antoine softly repairs the inside of a hairnet.

4.

Tonight I'm willing to admit a need for vices like
this reason for crossing Nevada without crisis.
Brief epitome of a life, you're not on the menus
of god, grow anemic in slits like the light of Italian
cinema. Only now a machine that comforts me
arrives in a box from the coast. Only now melted
peppermints, missed appointments, malice in a mosh pit.

5.

Ravishment in a dented van, a hamstring damaged
in the tenth inning. Antoine of the abnormal torso,
employee of the night, dirty in the retina
(not a Titan, not a Tibetan monk), whose impossibly
smooth unsmiling mouth disassembles me.

FLOWER OF THE HOUR

I wanted evil, doom, antechambers, dawns.

Didn't know who you were or why perhaps.

Soft fractals and scenarios flitted by.

You were Lady Earthly in an exile's café.

Paraphrase yourself and please sit still.

In the quiet part of disquiet I made a pact.

Annulled my nostalgia for flowers, louche

and fruitless. In the superfluous salon

of autumn, had no map of your malaise.

Whether "how are you?" or "gasps & screams."

IDEAS OF IDAHO

Even pheasants are phantasms in this tableland,
left off nesting, bereft of leaves, as a metal collar
tightens about the throat, a trigger, skin glistening
in the vista, you, in a foreground of feathers of dead
pheasants, Twin Falls a torsion of white before
the scope, tarnishing, in winter, as the year dies off
like fowl, a doe breathes lungfuls of her last minutes
of volition, the desert is dimension, land of bondage,
looking away, lucid against the truck's grime and rust,
you hold the crux of cross hairs steady, and I wait for
sheets of rain to drain these rituals of meaning,
the deed not done will die inside me *(this was the real
annihilation of our past)*, cold as a petrochemical
stain spreading south outside the nightclub, the sound
of your voice both cordial and corrosive in the foggy
felted wool of a windless day, gleam of skin in hunting
season, nights will be *mercy, mercy* in the metal
stitches of victims, the sun will become an obsession.

IDEAS OF OREGON

I was told to expect October, bulbs of orchids waiting overnight,
wapiti leaping down a gorge of granite after breeding season,
skin sloughed off, scant rainfall. Wapiti vaulting tines of cedar
after hunting season, outside the silver city gleaming in its
stitches, *what can be smashed must be smashed*, skinless, bare
of ornament, the battle over and the road to Portland covered
in snow, no one breathing nearby. Silence invades the house
like a Cossack, maestoso, minutely nerved, while you sleep off
your sleeplessness, renouncing daylight and its damages, the nightclub's
chemical glow. *I would not damage the skin in breeding season.*
Let creeping mistletoe & thorn be like our thoughts, like
velvet wires, at variance— as I watch myself watching you in late
November light, uttering things that people usually keep
to themselves *(tonight will be crevice or strife)*, preparing to leave
in that *I came I saw I conquered* dress of yours. (I thought there
was a book for everything.) In January, beneath a fascia of snow,
the earth will be faceless, inert, dawn will scatter over the freeway
like smashed headlights, (shortwave, shockwave, because *love
is obscene*), in January, when your hand leaves my hand,
in a mad bout of disbelief I will say *yes*— I will let go—

IN SQUIRE PARK WITH M., ESQUIRE

Summer finally lies facedown
in the red leaves of the equinox.

Beneath a nail-colored sky a shell-
shocked girl taunts me like a planet

with an iron core. She's always
changing her face, breathless

as a god-besotted pamphleteer
making her bed in some other,

less plastic world. We will never
know the implications of rhetoric

in this place of rife ephemera.
For days I dream we are

a euphoria of fused parts, love's
Trojan horse welcomed recklessly

into a recluse heart, beating,
then not beating, the river coursing

southward out of sight. The wind
carries no part of the park to me,

no weeds white as cartilage studded
with bells of dew. Vetch underfoot,

feverfew, a sense of either/or
in the trove of shadows. Her look

of lassitude is not a mask.
She is mine. I must not touch her.

BEYOND FLUORESCENCE

Soon this place will go strange on us in the white
afterglow of electrical storms, the skin of winter,

in the Dämmerung of a power outage, I dream
of downed wires and the picked locks of neighbors'

homes and all the houses on the street where I live,
the bars on windows, the sense of threat and death,

because when slag glows on the outskirts of town,
it burns all the hands that come near it, all the eyes,

wildflowers, all things that fire hurts are hurt by it,
even insects lose their wings and float down flooded

ditches. Soon there will be no one but strangers to take
our place because somewhere at the end of this place

is another place where animals materialize by the highway,
where no one will know why you went when you left

that morning with no license or address, your face already
roughened by the moon, umber leaves, with a madness

for anonymity, at the edge of a hint of a garden, no laws
to follow, gleaming, towards the Northern horse latitudes,

past the cattlebrown of cornfields, beyond fluorescence
and leather, beginning to renounce what you had stolen,

leaving alluvial deposits of land to fence and feathergrass,
forgetting fires that burned, glass that broke in your hand.

✦

ii.

FAREWELL TO FINALITY

Unbolt the terminal opus: an eon nosedives
into sepulchral green as a vexed engineer,

crooked by his printer, mulls over his crabbed

elysian plots, obscure as the sound of quail
slipping through the ashen grassland in arcs.

The gleaning is complete, the fleece he desired,

the flawed cast-off harness held by the hands
of a farmer at nightfall. In the barn, wind-

dried, sinister things, flasks of rye, sterile

pipes, rust-flowers, or, in the lusterless bulkhead
of a train weighed down with its cargo of bad

consequences, corn and its small grains in stasis,

shelled entities, barrows, commodities of other
countries, their kinky and promethean metals—

for as long as it takes, it is immaculate, inside,

the enormous horde of what is. Grease, *Geist*,
trenchers, a sealed alloy of paradox. How swiftly

the LCD in daylight goes pale where the unfinished

symphony leaves a defect, a fleck of green
in the snow of abstinence from noise that fuses

a mass of objects the engineer will never measure.

NOTE ON CROWS

Waking up cold below a profile
of crows, I cover the parts

of ailing trees, plinths & pediments,
for the ascent inside, I clear

a density of tentacles and wait by
the river for more flocks of crows.

In snow-marbled mud, they stamp skies
of shipwreck with opacities of clouds.

Everything is licked by a wind chime's
diverging tongues. The river comes

in the night like a corruption
that keeps demanding tentacles,

such a little night comes and,
sensing the attack, I wait for it.

WHAT HAS BEEN WEATHERED
HAS NOT BEEN WARDED OFF

December's paramour carries a briefcase
downstairs, fear like a piston gleaming in her face.

But she can speak & she would speak:
flies gather where abandonment happens.

All month she husbands their wings
until her version of reality is a wall I need

to destroy so sparrows can fly into it.
She would speak & she would not let

the Lords of Plastic deny the bullets
that rip into them, the day-glo saints

negating slugs, volts from broken wires.
Small as a doll in December, all month

she is darker by a mile of cambric than I,
injurious puppet, mercurial twin.

Night breaks up into small boards, shingles,
and the dangers of the sea are nearby.

Wireless transistor radio world,
she would speak through you & she will.

ALOOF FROM ALL THE MOORINGS, AND AFLOAT

Night is a door into possible dolor
down by the river where I stagger

into the calico leaves of late September
ending in a weather of rawness

and fluoxetine. Down by the river
where the best summers have gone by,

a stranger simultaneously darkens
the leaves of late September and stores

the data of their raindrops. Her analysis
of reality darkens inside me: *Hello,*

so I'm thinking of you. Though pain's
intrinsic to this place, I wake to find a nurse

dragging me up the Alps of epinephrine.
I leap from the impossible to the semiotic:

class is to *calla lily* is to *Eli Lilly.*
I pass under a trestle's pylons, thinking

of the brainwaves of those in pain,
of sirens, dialectics, and days long past.

The rationality I woke up with goes cold
as some brute staggers into a personality.

MICRO-THOUGHT ON A FLAT SURFACE

By the time I ride your horse through a rumor
of torture, you've already sickened. A government

thrown backward into a porphyry-colored hour
of occident and nocturne and a Dark Age doctrine

of causes can survive the harvest of machine guns
fired long ago only via weightlessness. Someone

must know why, blown by winds out of a crater,
dark markings, stars rich in europium, the sea cannot

be otherwise than here. If sensations are like geese
flying into guy wires, bright regions, rifts immense

as mouths of giant squid, what radio will tell us
news of the lack of purchase in this fissured field?

ONTOLOGICAL WEATHER

An April of interiors boils down to this: those who discover

the armed forces of the *I*. Latex, playgrounds, plastic visors.

A star/a density/a sky established by what's behind the eyes

that look at it. Spiders attach themselves to what takes place

in space with its color of retreating bodies. Threatened by

annulments of color, trees gain a toehold in the seamless crepe

of space. Quantities of fragments do not fray interior facts.

For those who posit structure as a thing that moves the world

in moving us, surfaces do not attach to what trembles as it

takes place, god's become a sobriquet for supreme nothingness.

Morning's a continuation of green bulbs barely seen, minnows

unstitching the river's Silurian gray, weeds shaped like asterisks

clumped together, referring to nothing. Inside a fact the color

of grape-frost the fringes of heresy grow. *You are/whom you*

have entered. Others softly become nobody outside in the grass.

VARIATIONS ON A THEME BEGINNING WITH DARKNESS

Darkness begins with the wrong
information, begins with flies
from carnage in a tar-patched road,
halters, neon diners, cowboy bars,

the river wrapped like a scarf
around the city's neck. At Lucky's
or the Red Horse Tavern, darkness
begins with *what's worse is…*

A lifelong study of the luster of flags
was Lucky's chivalrous enterprise.
The etiology of darkness is
nobody's home. The darkness

of money begins with *skill*
and ends in *douceur*—begins
with a bible and ends with a bribe.
Darkness, like boats on the ocean.

At Lucky's, a horse starts from
the doorway in which you made
a mistake, darkness starts with
imprecations, a glitter of cops,

thunderstorms. A mistake in inventory
becomes the darkness in which
you confess to wearing a scarlet
dress at the dark end of a bar.

The asphalt darkness of the road
to Lucky's cannot be overstated.
The cracked tar starts from nascent
mistakes in the paving. Darkness

starts from the ghost of a neon
sign where halter and horse are
polluted. *Let darkness be imbrued
luster.* In the lobby to which we repair…

THE VOODOO THAT YOU DO

Dolls understand the pseudo-problems
of zombies—their devices are *dresses,*
daylight, and *dialogue.* Dolls siphon off
the subject, feeding its dreams with chiffon.
They teeter on the edge of windows into
which we insert consciousness, false hopes
for a new museum, false hopes for dawn.
Polystyrene dolls can only map inputs
of extreme summer, the taxidermed,
torqued pelt of a fox behind plexiglas.
The zombie into which daylight erupts is
the surface where death becomes a given.
Dreams are massive temples of experience
into which zombie philosophers irrupt.

THE READER AS OBSERVER

Your ambivalence suggests that art
may be without its odd gifts, akin
to a ruined opera—its notes…its notes
might lighten into a Marxism that includes
a narrative of weather patterns of the world,
the prelude not so much to sexual identity
and rot and treefrogs breeding in water
but to the disappearance of sexual identity as
a problem. You try to remember the sky
without the gestations of a series of crimes,
an opera, its notes an unwholesome
deconstruction of the genre, and outside
the fog disclosing one of many inaccessible
roads. However, let it be said that the tires
of your car imply the color of the wet terrain.

ART AS SUBDIALECTIC

There is a glitter of evidence in all that is expression.
The moon, that sterile Petri dish, is cracked.

You may be the object of dreams of violence,
but any number of theories can be carried off

into the pines. The land riddled with leaves
is intrinsic to the main theme of night when

night is interpolated into a reading of the leaves.
And who are you, with closed car windows tinted?

All the boys may be blond in the spring, but you
can't have them; for now rain on the West End Bridge

leaves you unintelligible beneath the constellations,
the sky pushed back like old flannel. The river's name

comes to you as you leave the city's steel enigmas
(these yellow streets held you once, every last atom)

in the last taxi going north into Neolithic browns
of numberless leaves, *praxis* lapsing into *theoria*—

MEMENTO MORI: NIGHT MOTH

Trouble is a nimbus around what numbs
us to what could be, the city a package

wrapped in silver trees and streamers
of lights and ice that you unwrap as you

fly through it. As the city fades into clots
of grainy fog, sirens wail towards

an accident, and no phone will bring you
closer, the bad news crackling and the night

softening around you like the viscera
of the sick animal you have suddenly become:

the next morning is brine, ice cakes, blue screens
flashing beneath evergreens as cinder-colored

dots disperse, then tighten into a mask you wear
as you mount the steps of the county courthouse,

watching filaments scramble and unfold
themselves into trees while the lights of the city

below become chokecherries, crab apples,
polka dots, nothing you can eat, your voice

a deck of cards you shuffle and reshuffle
until you no longer comprehend or hear yourself.

iii.

✦

DEAR BEEKEEPER,

you have a way of listening
to rain that deadens questions completely.

I want to witness all the red
economies of venom in the first bee

whose memory survives inside
you as you arrive at the ornate

only to find it impoverished,
utterly bloodless bees mating linear

perspective with dead flies &
a vague yellow stain of summer,

solitary bees staring blandly into
all sorts of nothingness wherefore

other bees entirely mute are
a mathematical success

as evening spills over with honeybees,
an exquisite brownish gloom.

ARCHIVES OF BEES

As evening—

the ultimate end-user of the bee—erases today's
edition of *The Times*

once again I descend into archives, lost
contracts with clients, once again in enemy country,

everywhere my messages
lost by *messieurs* lost over and over

while nighttime waits for an offending *Instead*...

This involves many different brands
of perfume, a tube of Compound X,

histamines fore & aft, one cell floating
oceanward, a protein or two,

a need to look out the window &

your eyes, chicken farms, workers
brushing tiny numbers off their skin.

THE SILENCE OF BEES

Information opens for us a fen where dark juices
work their way through bridal hymns. I plant

a seed beside you and blow wishes in its direction.
(No one's at home in the azaleas.) Nighttime's

nearby like a dug-up grave. The moon spreads
its blueprints on the lawn of the institution

as evening comes in the form of thousands of bees.
The silence of a bee is in me as darkness inches

toward the ash plants. While others are away at mass,
I gather the leavings of bees. All night I wait for

morning's astounding crate of bees, full of deep
salty hours in which prairies concede their horizons.

CRITIQUE OF THE METAPHYSICS OF BEES

I.

Bees are tactile spots of disbelief in a field of air. The idea of them
is almost exhilarating. Amid the dogwoods of nearby suburbs,
banks in acute distress are closed. Phenomena in the wake of those
who are cold become pellucid. The principle of a held breath is no
more a god than a person altered by existence. Emergence into
existence is merely a fragment of a breath of god. I watch frag-
ments of red reveal parts of the water, remembering winter and the
end of white on page 11.

II.

The wintry faculty of white-on-white and what men it took away.
Hours after the knowledge of night is wasted on the distant,
luminous goal of the streets, we are stars reverberating in a conduit
like spokes of god. Those who seek to give shape to the Delphic day
find themselves dreaming, as it were, in the dark, gazing on a body
of changes and the stains of reeds (see *Bees*, 1979, 123). Descartes
left us with water and the languorous roar of lawnmowers starting
up in the distance.

III.

The subject wastes itself night after night over the sheer metallic
surface of its sense of self. Animals are primary and make no sense.
The creek demonstrates that if you wait, desires will shape your
body hour by hour. For weeks, to a surprising degree, I don't know
how much I dream in the dark. In the pharmacies of nearby
suburbs, sugarcane and bees are medication. This, if true, seems to
go beyond a bee's mere role-playing of an oblivious bee in its hive.

IV.

If I don't know of a passion, that is progress.

V.

The ways that bees behave do not admit of ruling principles. In assuming control of the world, you are not the body's best prospect but you are a body. Even a held breath hasn't a god's passivity (see *Hours & Nights*, 1992, 5). How can I vanish if I choose not to? Bees are not ours because we think of them.

VI.

The body wastes itself passively in the presence of illness. I concede to someone else the spruce that lends its presence to the creek. For weeks, and melodramatically, I don't describe what my dreams are in the dark. At any rate, at 5 am the government thinks my thoughts for me.

VII.

One's body or one's beehive bodily, one's thoughts, or one's think-ing the air is filled with thoughts. Take the dream of a new ac-quaintance in the dark. These offices change so oft the body profits, changes its rows into columns, changes its rose into—the bees have given grace a double winter.

VIII.

Due to the presence from which I exile myself, whose influence is thine and born of thee, of others' works for weeks I don't stomach the style—so oft have I found thee a Muse of fair profusion.

IX.

And every alien light in which you became pellucid. And every mind that goes numb in the suburbs. To these the bees, heavily tactile, sing.

X.

With sweetness in the dark my body changes. The stains of all my art succeed my body by the light of those who live in nearby suburbs. Hours after night wastes itself above the dark tactile spots of graves, the graves will aid our memory. The air, time's dial, thievish winter, and a bee's stealth may we know. The spruce lends its presence to what it cannot contain near the river where stars fall down like glass bees.

✦

iv.

✦

THE UNSAID

glitter of it, how like
paper flowers the birds

that emerge from this
purgatory of a neighborhood

the color of twilight not even
children were born to

an orange moon among pigeons,
poison figs, sun-crossed,

shrouded, what festers
in a dark dewy fattened

lobe of nightshade,
weightless flowers that

smell of some country
we were meant to wake into

CITY OF SURFEIT/CIRCUIT CITY

Welcome to my Helvetica font size 14 fantasy,
note the deranged circuitry— It may be that tonight

is just like last night, yet dead trees become architecture
haunting the dreams of manufacturers of networks

of input strings. *Welcome to the difference between*
navigable links and poisoning yourself with fear

in the face of wrapped parcels, false teeth. Night
transmits its technical dimensions and the rain

is compliant. Salesmen, standing frozen in friar's
black like petroglyphs in places people flee, imagine

birds flying through endless revisions of skies,
rain in a world retrofitted for floating menu links.

SHADOWBOXING

Sawtoothed clouds chew up a sky of chintz.

Watching the dumb show of people moving
through the streets of Vegas, all pantomimes

and itching palms, we loiter in the parking lot,
thinking *no one is alive enough to live here.*

Shadows slant down the side of the pawnshop
where a fire burned last month: where it teemed,

verboten, flowerlike, a small piece in the pageant
of the Nevermore & Shall-Remain-Nameless.

Sawdust clouds churn in a sky of quince.

Telephone poles stand still as a line of suspects
waiting in the wings not talking, holding out.

A man limps toward the husk of an opera house
dark as the city in its fishnet stockings of smog,

and we envy the ones who got away.
The sky gone smooth as a man's blue vein—

the one condemned *in absentia*—the world
left behind like a small coin on a dresser.

3 CAR GARAGE

What kind of chord or guttural mew of a thrush
thrown up on the shore where stakes groom
hard the brushed nickel trim of the sea's edge—

then, like downspouts of rainwater, what ghosts
our doors as epilogic as shadows that flourish
across some town of little or no population

—as rudders guide an aircraft over the plains…
we will not escape together. You talk of rockets,
voyeuristic views of outer space, with feedback

for the feeding of the multitudes reflected in some
walked-on water not to be forgotten, but listed
as a type of infrastructure needing overhaul and soon

to be outsourced. And you—*I wouldn't dare forget
you*—across the field, metal-cleated as if concrete
piles were nothing but old pencils, as if a vessel

snubbed at harbor, scuttled open by seacocks, traffic-
hindered, honeycomb of electrodes blown soft
as September apples imploding, a tomboy speeding

in a Cutlass Supreme beyond the blind arcades,
maritime tattoos blooming across biceps, dream-
peddled, past the dumbstruck on the village green.

AN ÉCORCHÉ OF THE CONTINENT

Let me sketch in for you the mayhem of last year's
passion by which the world was morally bleached.
So began my immersion in the attenuated darkness
of carnivals. In the battle for this virtual circa-1980
city the things we get into get out of hand. Beneath
your morality lies a muted elsewhere where all
the world's gear systems fall apart. Thank you for
all the pretty toxins but promise me we'll find a way
to wake up when it's time. Married to a businessman
in Lower Manhattan, you mimicked the feelings
of a ruined queen, cognate of vast spaces supervened
by mythologies. Considering what you were made
from is nothing malformed? My office overlooks
a hillside of UV rays, marshland, *mersclond*, Proto-
Germanic fen, a morning vaguely interlaced with
cinematic moons, staccato shapes of dying men.
Thank you for gestures too priceless to believe.
Whole cities die of too much space inside them.

THRILLSVILLE

When the mind begins to see the lies it loves
with eyes that could have looked elsewhere,
old pain repullulates. Errors of architecture,

errors of eros, the train ride out is not
the train ride in. Is this the kind of life
you left us for? No one has a face in the dark.

Needles keep pulling away from their source
in the spruce, manganese, more ascetic angles,
without danger to the traveler who goes back home

and finds a dog digging a hole in the yard,
cells multiplying in the veins of the sick.
Even now, when the city is dark, I get lost

without you—you who would deceive
yourself with oracles, with flawed mechanics,

though the weatherman predicts rain in April,
tractors lurk like malignant growths in the fields
of soybeans outside of town and the town itself

is a necropolis of wrought iron gates. This is how
your heart is—needles behind, needles before.
No one gets to keep the face they came here with.

PHANTOMS OF UTOPIA

Out in the streets, the phantoms of utopia
are darkening, tangling their hair

in waveforms, turning bitter.
The fog they feared has become colossal.

They've been doing the same thing for years now
and no new data. Still the pig iron

and smelted steel drift in on a barge
from Guatemala. Still the cars

carry their smells onto highways.
Those cars are not like ships on the sea.

The radars are there, invisible schemes
and frequencies, without odor or color or need.

Through exotic reticulations of trees
they send their strange intelligence.

Out in streets full of barbiturates,
the phantoms of utopia are seeking the historical

in florid landscapes, splayed flowers,
fondly arranged limbs. All day

they appear to be cultivating their thoughts
and the delicate, plantlike extensions

of their thoughts. *Goodbye fine rain falling,
goodbye idea of the good.* Outside,

daylight is blue against spruce trees
and a dead girl lives again in your memory,

sunlight a broth breaking over her mouth,
a breath, why DNA, why anything?

At dusk, the phantoms of utopia
close the doors to their houses

as if increments of evil were veiled
in the fog that haunts them. The reproach

in their eyes makes you shy. Minus
an inner sanctum, they are like you.

FROM *THE DIALOGUE OF BALM*

As the city grows old in an atmosphere of caskets
and glass, there is no balm of Gilead, no balsam

of Peru nor catharsis of tumor, bruise, catarrh—only
steel pylons, premium-grade, galvanized, carving

up the river, cold as the zinc mask of a joker's face,
as blank and bluish white. The house smells of loose-

strife, Floridian glades, an old man's aftershave.
Outside the city in whose soil so many soldiers lay,

sunlight blooms like a dropped bomb, schoolboys
collect comic books and tattoo art in a landscape

of brownstone and sepia, a landscape of lost causes/
casus belli. No new world wind makes a noise

in the weathervane. Out of the bucolic green
of the belle époque, trains stagger like bad dreams,

bearing their bloodlessness into the *o* of paroxysm.

platelets of fog folding into others
perversely motionless. In Flint, Michigan,
I saw unfolding from a parlor your
skin's unholy hue. Among constellations
of shades, another frantic hemlock no-
thing. *I wish your mouth a manifold of
this.* It gets in here. Is no cracked Adriatic.
Will not be steady between stilled thighs.
Most without reason you entered
whence is no man nor Chinese lantern.

BOMBER'S MOON

Rainfall at night is the color of foxgloves,
of death in the roots. It falls on the cube-
shaped cabins, cold as a dream of autumn.

No one monitors the cold, and for the next
several years you will lose the beauty
of the strangeness of your face in the fences

of a new empire. Deadlocked in this private zone
of pine trees, its long dereliction of trailer courts

and old motels, you drop a stone down a well,
make a wish on the polestar, as if the last thousand
lunations had never been. But no one can take

the stain from the osprey's nest. As if offended
by the light of a bomber's moon, you entertain
the cedars with the achromatic matrix of your face.

MARGINS AND MEMBRANES

Whether those are birds or bats flying
in the burned sky, whether the margins
of Main Street look maimed among the tiny
physiologies of trillium and hawkweed
as the sky goes from the color of the sea
to the color of something rotting, you
stay below the sheriff's radar, south
of the Miracle Wash, the Kash n' Karry,
where birds abide, petrochemicals
in their blood, while nightcrawlers twist
like fingers in the mud, as the sky is salted
with stars equal parts alien and mundane,
and the day's membranes bloom into

a *raison d'etre.*

PERFECT MOTELS

When a bird dies
it falls through the air
like the ending of the sublime.

I read all day
until fireflies start
out of livid places

and trouble the twilight
like candles in the windows
of a woman's home

flickering *I'm here*
I'm here to anyone
who will see.

At five o'clock,
as if the sun were a thought
in a thinker's mind,

some master passion
of a taciturn heart,
I am of two minds,

suspending things
in small nacreous
twilights of consciousness.

Take anything
to the nth degree
and it dismantles you.

After so many movements,
small wonder
a thing must die.

To alterations blue
and phenomenal as this sky,
I wake at midnight,

keeping things I
remember close
at hand and disquieting.

✦

✦

NOTES:

"How Many Cool Hundreds": "I am a god, rising,/ the chips of blue plastic fly" is an echo of a line in Plath's poem "Fever 103º." Chuck-a-luck is a dice game in which players bet on certain configurations of numbers appearing on the dice.

"Boolean Conditions": The phrase "artists in violence who build states" is from Nietzsche's *The Genealogy of Morals*, Second Essay, section 18.

"Ideas of Idaho": The lines "this was the real/annihilation of our past" are a slightly altered version of a sentence in Patricia Highsmith's novel *The Talented Mr. Ripley*. The phrase "both Cordial and Corrosive" is from George Herbert's "Sighs and Groans."

"Ideas of Oregon": The phrase "creeping Mistletoe & Thorn" is from William Blake's "The Ghost of Abel." "What can be smashed must be smashed" was the ultimatum of Russian nihilist Dmitri P. Pisarev.

"What Has Been Weathered Has Not Been Warded Off": The title and the phrase "*But she can speak and she would*" are modified versions of phrases written by Joe Wenderoth in a letter published in *American Poetry Review*, Jan./Feb. 1995.

 "Aloof from All the Moorings, and Afloat": The title comes from Emerson's essay "Intellect" from the *Essays: First Series*. In context it reads as follows: "He in whom the love of truth predominates will keep himself aloof from all moorings, and afloat. He will abstain from dogmatism, and recognize all the opposite negations, between which, as walls, his being is swung."

"Micro-Thought on a Flat Surface": The title phrase is from the essay "What Is a Document?" by Michael K. Buckland.

"Ontological Weather": Line 10 is from Leszek Kolakowski's *Metaphysical Horror,* as follows, " 'God' becomes a sobriquet for the supreme Nothingness of the Absolute." The statement *"You are/ whom you have entered"* was influenced by a passage in Elizabeth Willis' *The Human Abstract.*

"The Silence of Bees": Line 9 echoes a line in Seamus Heaney's poem "In Memoriam M.K.H., 1911-1984" from *Clearances:* "When all the others were away at Mass…"

DEL SOL PRESS, based out of Washington, D.C., publishes exemplary and edgy fiction, poetry, and nonfiction (mostly contemporary, with the occasional reprint). Founded in 2002, the press sponsors two annual competitions:

THE DEL SOL PRESS POETRY PRIZE is a yearly book-length competition with a January deadline for an unpublished book of poems. The judge for 2004 was Reginald Shepherd, and the contest winner was Julianne Buchsbaum's *A Little Night Comes.*

THE ROBERT OLEN BUTLER FICTION PRIZE is awarded for the best short story, published or unpublished. The deadline is in November of each year.

Full guidelines and more information are available on the website:

HTTP://WEBDELSOL.COM/DSP

✦

JULIANNE BUCHSBAUM is the author of *Slowly, Slowly, Horses* (2001, Ausable Press). She is currently a Ph.D. candidate in English and Creative Writing at the University of Missouri-Columbia.